SEND ME
Wings

Bobby Cyrus

ISBN 978-1-0980-1622-7 (paperback)
ISBN 978-1-0980-1623-4 (digital)

Christian Faith Publishing, Inc.
832 Park Avenue
Meadville, PA 16335
www.christianfaithpublishing.com

Printed in the United States of America

Ron and Sarah Boggs live in Charleston South Carolina. They are both retired. Although they are only in their early fifties. They never had any children so they both were really focused on their careers. Ron was a civil engineer and Sarah worked as an accountant following in the footsteps of her father. When the couple were first married they had a plan and they followed it with perfection. Especially Ron! Ron was very driven by the stock market and investing. He set a goal and achieved it. There are times he can seem a little too passionate about the financial things in life. But overall Ron is a very solid Christian man who is head over heels in love with his wife and when it comes to Sarah he has the patience of Job. Sarah was an only child to Bob and Judy Thompson. As I mentioned before she followed in her father's footsteps and worked as an accountant. Sarah is a very humble but strong woman. She is a little old fashion when it comes to Ron. You know the cooking, cleaning, tending to her man thing? I doubt you will ever hear Ron complain.

Ron's mother and father passed away many years ago as did Sarah's father. For the past several years they have been caring for Sarah's mother who endured a long battle with cancer. They were selfless care givers. Trying to make Judy as comfortable as possible. Sometimes Sarah would not even sleep during the night because she would be afraid she would not hear her call. That terrified her! Her mama told her many times to admit her in a nursing facility and she could come there and see her, and it wouldn't be so hard on Sarah. But Sarah knew her mother wanted to be home in her house. She felt with all she is going through at least she has all her things around her to give her comfort. Not to mention when the house was built Judy supervised every nail being driven and every brick being laid. Judy Thompson loved her home!

The sun was shining through the big bay window in the living room. You could feel a warm quiet peace throughout the house. They had moved Judy's bed close to that window, so she could see outside. The rain always gave her comfort and she said looking at the sun was like looking at the face of God. The morning of September 2, 2014 it was obvious Judy's battle was almost over. She looked beautiful and at peace as the sun rays warmed her blankets. She had no struggle and did not seem to have any pain. Later that afternoon she slowly and effortlessly took her last sweet breath.

PREFACE

This book was inspired by a song I wrote several years ago. I did not have an inspiration that caused me to write the song so I told my mother and father the first time they heard it that it must be a gift from God. I did not feel I was capable of writing such a story. I later shared this song with my cousin Billy Ray Cyrus and he was very moved by the lyrics and music, it stuck with him for years. So, many years later he and I were on the phone having a fairly deep, emotional conversation about life, God and legacy. In conversation Billy shared with me that he had been approached about starring in a movie for a major network. He said they had not chosen a script yet and asked him if he had a project he would like to submit. I was very excited for him and shared my enthusiasm. It was strange he and I had been on the phone so long that night, in the past our conversations were usually shorter. We both made comments making reference to this about an hour into the visit.

As I was sharing my excitement for him and his new opportunity with much emotion, he cut me off! He began to say "I now know why we have been on this call for so long. Send Me Wings!! Your song! That has to be the movie." I was shocked! I really did not know how to respond. So, before I could say much of anything, he said "Bobby, you have to write it." I said "Billy, I don't know how to write a movie script, I am a songwriter." He told me "The song came from you so, the story for the script has to come from you.". Of course, I was honored and mortified! I had no idea where to start but I accepted the challenge! My dad used to write Christmas plays for our church back in Kentucky so, I thought I would draw from those.

It is amazing what the internet can teach you about writing movie script too! That night I began and after 6 months of many tears and many hours I was finished. This project has been one of the most challenging and rewarding works I have created in my career.

A couple of years had gone by and the movie had not yet been put into production. So, I decided to find a way to share this with the masses. That is when I went on my quest to find a publisher who might take the time to read what I had written and help me make a dream and a story come to life. You will notice when you begin reading the book it is still in script form. I want you to read exactly the way I wrote it. There is much healing in this story. Some parts are hard to take in but if you believe, you will understand. Thank you for taking the time to read my work. I don't consider myself a novelist or playwright, I am a Country Boy from the hills of East Kentucky who was blessed with the gift of writing a song. I hope you enjoy my book and I pray that it may touch your life and in a positive way.

SCENE 1

Ron and Sarah Boggs are at home getting ready to go meet with an attorney. Sarah's mother has recently passed away.

Ron: Sarah, did Mr. Lyndsey give you any idea what is in your mother's will?

Sarah: No, but I can't imagine what it could be. We went through all her money taking care of her while she was sick, she took a reverse mortgage out on the house after dad passed away, and sold pretty much everything else.

Ron zips her dress and then she helps tie his tie.

Ron: Well maybe she had a Swiss Bank account that nobody knew about and we will be billionaires! *(Chuckles.)*

Sarah: Not likely! Dad was an accountant and Mom volunteered for different organizations and helped Dad during tax season. I was pretty spoiled with whatever I wanted since I was an only child. Somehow, I don't think it was quite enough to fill up a Swiss Bank account! *(laughs)* Sometimes I think that's all you think about! *(Chuckles.)*

Ron: I am just kidding around, honey! Seriously it is probably just some special heir loom that meant a lot to her. Hey, we better go or we gonna be late!

Ron and Sarah are walking in the attorney's office.

Sarah: Good morning!

Receptionist: Good morning. How can I help you?

Sarah: My name is Sarah Boggs, and this is my husband Ron. We have an appointment with Mr. Lyndsey.

Receptionist: Mr. Lyndsey, Mr. and Mrs. Boggs are here to see you. He said you could come on in. Here let me get the door.

Ron: Thank you!

Receptionist: No Problem. You are so welcome!

Ron and Sarah enter the office.

Mr. Lyndsey: Good Morning, Sarah! Good Morning, Ron!

Ron: Good morning, Mr. Lyndsey!

Sarah: Good morning, Mr. Lyndsey!

Mr. Lyndsey: Can I offer you something to drink? Coffee? Water?

Ron: No thank you. Had enough this morning to float a battle ship.

Mr. Lyndsey: How about you, Sarah?

Sarah: No I'm good.

Mr. Lyndsey: Really sorry about your mama. She was a fine lady! She was always trying to help others and she was one of the nicest people I have ever known. Well, *(Fumbling through some files.)*

here it is! Isn't funny when you are trying to find something it's always at the bottom of the pile or the last place you look.

Ron: *(Laughs.)* That is very true!

Sarah laughs. Mr. Lyndsey hands Sarah a folder.

Mr. Lyndsey: Here you go! Your mother's last and only possession.

Sarah opens the file and inside is a deed to a church and property in a small town in Virginia. She had a look of anguish on her face and was a bit agitated.

Sarah: Mr. Lyndsey, I thought she got rid of this years ago?

Mr. Lyndsey: Well, apparently, she decided to hang on to it and give it to you.

Ron: Let me see, Sarah.

Sarah: I wish she would have asked me if I wanted that old church!

She hands the file to Ron. Ron is reading the deed.

Ron: Where is Hopetown, Virginia?

Sarah: It was my hometown. We moved away from there when I was five years old. *(Sarah becomes anxious and ready to leave.)* Mr. Lyndsey, thank you for your time and the kind words you said about my mother! Please excuse us but we need to go.

Sarah grabs her purse and the file and walks out of the office quickly.

Mr. Lyndsey: Ron, I hope I didn't do anything to upset her!

Ron: No, no, absolutely not. She has just had a hard time with the loss of her mother. Sarah is not one to show her emotions to openly. Thank you again for everything. *(Shakes Mr. Lyndsey's hand.)* Have a great day!

SCENE 2

Ron exits the office and catches up with Sarah. On their way home they stop to have lunch.

Ron: I wonder what this property could be worth. You know, Sarah, one of the reasons we both retired early was to start our own business and spend more time together. This could be the ticket! This could be a God send!

Ron is very excited and optimistic about the inheritance. Sarah is quiet and playing with her salad with a fork not really talking and not really eating just deep in thought.

Ron: Hey, what's wrong?

Sarah: I'm sorry. This is just a lot to soak in one day. I just can't wrap my head around why Mom kept this land and that old church?

Ron: Well, maybe I am right? It may be a God send! Your mother may not have known why but she may have felt you would need it for something someday. You did say it is your hometown. I think we should drive up there and check it out. Then at least we will know what we have or what we don't have.

Sarah: I have not been back there since I was five years old. It's Christmas is in a couple of weeks.

Ron: All the more reason to go! Christmas in the mountains! Come on, Sarah, it might help to do something different this year. Hey, we may even run into one of your ol' boyfriends.

Sarah: *(Laughs sarcastically.)* I am sure we will. I started dating when I was three. It is probably beautiful this time of year with all the snow and Hopetown always went overboard with Christmas decorations.

Ron: *(lays money on the table for the bill.)* Sarah, this will be fun. A road trip might be a good thing for us. We have been so busy. It would be nice to get away from the norm for a few days!

Sarah: I know, I know it's just…

Ron: It's just what?

Sarah: Nothing—really nothing! This will be a good thing! Let's go! Who knows? We may be sitting on a gold mine!

SCENE 3

Ron and Sarah are driving in Ron's truck to a Hopetown, Virginia. They arrive at the edge of town and Sarah is looking in a tourist guide that she picked up on the way. Searching for a place to stay, she comes across a bed and breakfast that used to be an old house. They have arrived at the bed and breakfast.

Sarah: Well, this looks like the place. I think I remember this old house. They must have spent a fortune remodeling! If I remember right it was about to fall down when I was a kid.

Ron: *(Unloading luggage from the truck.)* What did you pack in this bag? *(Grunting.)*

Sarah: *(Standing beside the truck looking around about half listening to Ron.)* Shoes and stuff. Well, let's get checked in.

SCENE 4

They enter the bed and breakfast. An Elderly lady greets them at the door.

Alberta: Welcome, welcome, welcome! We are so glad you chose to spend your time with us while you are in town! Even though we are the only place in town! *(Laughs heartily.)* You folks must be worn out? How long was your drive?

Sarah: It was a pretty good hike! But the mountains are so beautiful it wasn't all that bad.

Alberta: Ted come in here and help these folks with their luggage

Ron: Thank you so much but I can handle it!

Alberta: Sweetie, *(As she looks at Sarah.)* you look just like a woman I used to know that lived in this town over forty years ago. Her name was Judy Thompson.

Sarah: That was my mother.

Alberta: Oh, dear lord! You're little Sarah! You look just like your mama! How is she these days?

Sarah: Mom passed away last month. She had been sick for a while.

Alberta: I am so sorry! She was such a sweet lady. (*Expressions of sorrow and ponders in thought for a moment.*) Well, what brings you back to your home town?

Sarah: Mom left me the old church and property.

Alberta: Really?! (*Strained look on her face.*) Well…

Sarah: I was shocked when the attorney handed me the file. I thought Mom sold it years ago!

Ron: We thought we would come up and check it out. We plan on preparing it to sell and use the money to start our own business back in Charleston, South Carolina. That is where we live.

Alberta: (*Kind of bewildered*) Sounds like you have a good plan… (*Alberta becomes excited again.*) Well it's good to have you back for whatever reason you're here! Here is your key and you have the best room in the house! Top of the stairs first door on your right!

Ron notices the awkwardness when the old church is mentioned. It made him think of when they were in the attorney's office and Sarah's reaction when she first saw the deed. They settle in their room and Ron is anxious to see the town.

Ron: Hey, let's stretch our legs and see the sights. It's still early and I could use some coffee and maybe a slice of good ol' homemade pie. I saw a little restaurant as we came in to town. It looks like they are decorating for Christmas! This has always been my favorite time of year.

Sarah: Me too! I remember when I was a little girl and Mom would let me stand on a bucket and help her bake Christmas cookies, pies and candy. Everything she Made was always so good! I told my friends her hands were magic and…(*Sarah sits on the edge of the bed and breaks down. Ron quickly wraps his arms around her and holds her while she cries.)* Ron, I miss her *so* much. Sometimes I think I hear her calling for me. She fought so hard when she was sick! One time she apologized to me for getting sick. *(Wiping tears from her eyes.)* She said she was so sorry that she had become such a burden. I wonder sometimes if I made her feel that way. Did I act frustrated or say something to make her think like that?

Ron: Sarah, you were her guardian angel. Your mother was one the sweetest most caring people that I have ever known. Her saying that to you is just who she was and a true testament of her love for her daughter.

As they embrace affectionately Ron helps dry her tears and gives her a soft kiss.

Sarah: I love you so much.

Ron: And I love you so much. Now, how about some good ol' home-made mountain pie?

Sarah: *(Big smile.)* Sounds good to me!

SCENE 5

Ron and Sarah are walking down the sidewalk admiring the decorations. They both notice something that seems odd.

Sarah: The decorations are beautiful, but I don't see anything really about the baby Jesus?

Ron: I noticed that too. You see Christmas trees, lights everywhere, Santa Claus, but no nativity scenes or anything that represents the birth of Christ.

Sarah: Kind of eerie.

Ron: Hey, there's the diner I saw!

Sarah: I remember that place. We would eat there sometimes after church on Sunday. I can't believe it is still open!

SCENE 6

They are sitting in the Diner looking at the menu.

Peggy Jean: Well now, welcome to Johnny's Burgers and Pies. We have the best burgers in Virginia and the most delicious home-made pies your tongue will ever taste! *(Sassy laugh.)* So what can I get you folks?

Sarah: I will have water and coffee with a piece of apple pie.

Ron: Uh… I would like coffee and a slice of your blackberry pie.

Peggy the waitress can't take her eyes off Sarah while she is getting their drinks and pie. She goes back to their table with a curious look on her face.

Peggy Jean: Sweetie, you look really familiar to me? Are you from here?

Sarah: I was born here but moved away when I was five years old.

Peggy Jean: What is your name?

Sarah: My name is Sarah Boggs. Well, I used to be Thompson.

Peggy Jean: Sarah Thompson?! Oh my goodness! We used to play together when we were kids. I am Peggy Pack! I lived across the street from you!

Sarah: I remember you. You were little Miss Apple Fest. I was so jealous when I saw you in the parade. *(They both laugh.)* Where did time go?

Peggy Jean: Well, you see where that crown got me! *(More laughter.)* By the way how is your mama?

Sarah: *(Sarah looks at Ron and out the window for a brief moment then looks a Peggy.)* We lost mom a little over month ago.

Peggy Jean: I am so sorry! I lost my mama last year. *(A moment of reflection from both.)* Well, what in the world brings you back to this podunk town?

Sarah: Mom left the old church to Ron and me. We thought we would come up and check it out and probably prepare it to sell.

When Sarah mentions the old church the diner became awkwardly quiet. A couple of people turn around and look her way.

Peggy Jean: Wow! Nobody's mentioned that place in years. *(Peggy seems to be in brief deep thought then shakes her head.)* Well, it's good to see you again Sarah and good luck with everything. You better watch that handsome husband of yours around here or these ol' mountain girls may try to steal him.

Ron notices again the strange reaction from people when the old church is mentioned. He doesn't say anything to Sarah. But he is becoming very curious.

Ron: *(As they finish and pay the bill.)* Let's run by the church and take a look before dark.

Sarah: It's getting pretty late.

Ron: We won't get out. We'll just drive by. I promise!

Sarah: As long as we are just driving by. I am exhausted!

Scene 7

They are in the truck pulling up in front of the old church. Ron roles down the window and is looking around and making comments about things to do. Sarah is in a deep stare at the church not hearing a word cut Ron says. She looks pale and scared with a very troubled look on her face.

Ron: Man, it looks pretty rough, but I can hire a couple of local boys and cut all the brush, fix that old fence, and just clean up around the church. We can make a burn pile of old wood and brush in that field in the back. I am pretty sure that is part of the deed. *(Ron is getting no response from Sarah and turns and looks at her.)* Hey, Sarah, are you okay?

Sarah: Yeah, I think it may have been the pie not agreeing with me. I just feel a little sick to my stomach. Let's go back to the bed and breakfast and get some rest. We can do this tomorrow.

Ron: Of course! Hey, we are not on a schedule anyway.

SCENE 8

The next morning Ron is very anxious to get moving! Sarah is reluctant to commit to going out to the property.

Ron: *(Talking through the bathroom door.)* Sarah, are you about ready?

Sarah: Just a minute.

Sarah comes out of the bathroom.

Ron: Hey, you ready to go? I want to get an early start.

Sarah: I was thinking that I should probably go to the courthouse and make sure there are no back taxes or liens filed on the deed. I would hate for us to find a buyer and then run into an issue. I would rather resolve any of those issues before we put it on the market.

Ron can sense a hesitation with Sarah about going to the property. He is convinced that there is something to all the awkwardness and Sarah's reluctant behavior towards the Church. He does not push the issue. Ron is a very patient man.

Ron: That's a good idea! You never know after all these years. Okay, I will head on out there and develop a plan to move forward.

Sarah: Okay, honey. Have a great day and call me if you need anything.

SCENE 9

Ron is sitting on the tailgate of his pickup truck in front of the old church when the town sheriff pulls up.

Sheriff: Good morning. My name is H. R. Tanner. I guess you could call me the law in these parts.

Ron: Good morning, Sheriff. My name is Ron Boggs.

Sheriff: Glad to meet you, Mr. Boggs. Don't mean to be nosy. Just not used to seeing people stop by this old church.

Ron: Is that right? My wife just recently inherited this property from her mother. We drove up to check it out and to prepare it to put on the market.

Sheriff: Wait a minute. You sayin' you're married to little Sarah Thompson?

Ron: Well she was a Thompson until she married me and now she's a Boggs. Did you know them?

Sheriff: Well, in a small town like this everybody knows everybody. I sure hate to hear that about Sarah's mother. I knew her father had passed away a few years back. Bob and Judy were good folks. I imagine it was really hard for them to get over what happened in this old church. I'm sure Sarah has told you all about it.

Ron: Well, Sheriff, since you brought it up, I didn't even know that this was Sarah's hometown until we met with the attorney the other day. When Mr. Lindsey the attorney gave Sarah the folder with the deed to the property, she became very upset, anxious, and seemed agitated. When we arrived at the bed and breakfast last night, Sara mentioned to the lady why we are here and brought up the old church. The lady seemed very awkward for a moment, almost like she was afraid to respond. Then we went to a little diner down the street and the same thing happened there with the waitress and other folks that were in the diner.

Ron notices a little boy in a field behind the church.

Sheriff: Sounds like Sarah has kept this buried inside for way too long. Since it is your place you should know its history. *(Ron and the Sherriff sit on the tailgate of Ron's truck.)* Back in those days, the Johnson family lived a few miles out of town. The mother had passed away so her six boys and husband were left behind. The boys and old man Johnson were a rough sort always causing trouble around the county. An old, widowed woman lived not far from their place. Those boys had been stealing tools and farm equipment from her barn. Sometimes they would get wild on moonshine and drive their trucks through her garden and fields, destroying everything she had planted. Besides all the stealing and damage to her place she was scared that they would come in some night and hurt her. She reported it to the local sheriff many times. However, the sheriff was a cousin to the Johnson's so he never would respond to the complaints and just acted like the old, widow woman was just over-reacting. He would say that those boys were little wild but harmless…

Ron hears a call coming through on the sheriff's radio.

Ron: I hate to interrupt you, Sheriff, but I think someone is trying to reach you on your radio.

Sheriff starts walking towards his vehicle.

Sheriff: My goodness, I didn't even hear that. My wife has been after to me to get a hearing aid. I guess it's about time. *(Grabs radio mic.)* This is Sheriff Tanner. Go ahead. Over.

Dispatch: Sheriff, we just got a call. We have an 11-80 out on HWY 23. Sounds pretty bad, Sheriff.

Sheriff: Okay, dispatch! I am on my way! Mr. Boggs, I hate to cut our visit short, but there is a bad wreck and I am going to have to hurry!

Ron: Of course! I hope those folks are okay!

Sheriff: Me too! *(As he is pulling out.)* I will catch up with you in a few days and finish that story!

Ron: Sounds good, Sheriff.

Ron is noticing the little boy out behind the church as he is talking to the Sheriff. Ron sits back down on the tailgate of the truck. He is in heavy thought about the story the sheriff started telling him. The little boy behind the church seems to be on a mission. Ron notices him carrying wood out to the middle of the field. He becomes fixed on this boy and what he is constructing. After a while it looks like a ladder the boy is building. When the boy makes an attempt to climb the contraption it falls apart and he falls hard to the ground. Ron runs out to make sure he is okay.

Ron: Hey there, buddy, you okay? *(The boy is scooting on the ground away from Ron. He seems scared.)* My name is Ron. What's yours?

The boy just looks at him and stays silent. He is very skinny he also seems frail and is dark under his eyes like shadows.

Ron: Well, okay. Hey, little brother, you don't need to be scared. I am not going to hurt you. What were you trying to build with this old pile of wood anyway?

Jessie: Jessie

Ron: You mean your name is Jessie?

Jessie: Yes, sir, that is my name. I was trying to build a ladder.

Ron: Where were you expecting to climb to out here in the middle of a field?

Jessie: A place called Heaven.

Ron: Jessie, who told you that's how you get to Heaven?

Jessie: I found a book in that old house and it talked about a place called Heaven. It said that nobody was sad, there was no fighting, and no one could hurt you. It said a man called Jesus lives there, he loves everybody, and that Heaven was above the clouds. Truth is no one cares if I am here or not. So, I have been trying to find a way to get there.

Ron: *(Unsure of how to respond to the boy's comment.)* Well, Jessie, I am sure that your mama wouldn't want you to leave. I think you should keep reading that book and it may tell you how to get there. You're just a boy; you have got plenty of time to work out your journey to heaven. Now here, let me help you up. *(The little boy is standing in front of Ron.)* Jessie? Do you have a home to go to?

Jessie: Yes, sir, it's not far through the woods. Mr. Boggs, is this your old house?

Ron: Yes, it belongs to me and my wife, Sarah. But it actually used to be a church.

Jessie: I don't know nothing about no church.

Ron: I think you know more than you realize. So, your parents have never taken you to Sunday school?

Jessie: They don't have school around here on Sundays. Besides Mama stopped making me go to school when I was nine years old. She said it was too much trouble to fool with every day and all the teachers were stupid anyway.

Ron realizes that Jessie does not understand anything about going to church. He finds his conversation with Jessie curious and disturbing. Jessie starts walking towards a patch of woods at the edge of the field behind the church.

Ron: Hey, Jessie!

Jessie: Yes, sir?

Ron: Keep reading that book you found. It's got a lot of great stories in it. *(He smiles at Ron and continues to walk away.)*

SCENE 10

Sarah is at the courthouse.

Jo: Good morning. What can I help you with, mam.

Sarah: Hello. My name is Sarah Boggs and I need to speak to someone about checking on a piece of property for any owed taxes
or liens. I also will need to find out what I need to do as far
as transferring the deed into my name. *(Sarah is opening her
shoulder bag to get the folder.)* I inherited this property recently
and my husband and I are preparing it to be sold so I wanted to
make sure I have everything taken care of before we place it on
the market. Whew, finally! Here you go. I included my mother's
will for proof of inheritance.

Jo: Okay, let me see what we need to do. *(Looking through the papers.
Awkward amount of time goes by of silence between Sarah and Jo.)*

Sarah: Is there something wrong?

Jo: I will be right back. I need to check on something.

Sarah: Okay?

*Jo disappears in a back office. A few moments later an old gentleman, the
County Court Clerk, comes walking in.*

Mr. Hall: Good morning, mam. My name is Michael J. Hall. I am the County Court Clerk. And your name?

Sarah: Pardon me. My name is Sarah Boggs.

Mr. Hall: *(Stares at Sarah for a brief moment.)* I know who you are. I was a deacon in your grandfather's church.

Sarah: *(Sarah smiles.)* I remember you, Mr. Hall. My father was very fond of you. He spoke of you quite often. He said you were a man of great character and a true man of God.

Mr. Hall: Your Daddy was a fine man and a good friend. It really was hard to see all of you move away. But, considering the circumstances, we all understood. It was tough for the whole town but for your parents and you I can't imagine what you all have been through dealing with such a tragedy.

Sarah: *(Tears welling up in her eyes.)* Well, Mr. Hall, I have not done so well dealing with it. My husband and I have been married for twenty-four years and I have never told him what happened. Until the other day, at the attorney's office to read Mom's will, he had no idea this was my home town. I was shocked when I opened the folder and saw the deed. I thought Mom and Dad sold it years ago.

Mr. Hall: Well, Sarah, your mother may have thought leaving you this old church would somehow make you have to deal with it once and for all. She was always a strong woman, as I remember, and very practical.

Sarah: *(Wiping tears from her face.)* I am so sorry for being a cry baby, Mr. Hall. Seems like here lately that's all I do. *(Embarrassed and brief soft laugh.)*

Mr. Hall: Sarah, God gave us tears to help wash away the burdens that life lays on us at times. Everything happens for a reason. I don't think for a minute that your mother leaving this church to you was by accident.

Jo: Mrs. Boggs, I can't find anything against the property. As far as the deed, you will need to have an attorney handle that for you and then we can process it here at the clerk's office.

Mr. Hall: This is my granddaughter.

Sarah: Don't you have two boys? Hunter and Hayden?

Mr. Hall: That's a good memory!

Sarah: Jo, which one is your dad?

Jo: Hayden.

Sarah: *(Smiling.)* Your dad was an awfully handsome boy. He was a lot older than me, but I remember how cute he was. *(Jo laughs.)* What ever happened to Hunter?

Mr. Hall: He is a hunting guide and has a hunting show that airs all over the South. He is doing what he has always loved to do. Hey, where is Mr. Boggs?

Sarah: He is out at the church looking around to see what needs to be done to make it marketable. I kind of bailed on him. I am just not ready. He can sense something, but he hasn't said anything. He has noticed the reactions from everyone we have talked to since yesterday.

Mr. Hall: He sounds like a patient man. You'll have to bring him by before you leave town.

Sarah: Ron is a very humble and patient man. He has had to be to live with me. I will for sure bring him by.

Jo: Sarah, it was nice meeting you and good luck with the sale.

Sarah: It was nice meeting you too! Mr. Hall, thank you for speaking with me and thank you for the things you said. It makes me understand a little more why Mom didn't get rid of the church.

Mr. Hall: Your welcome, Sarah! Let me know if you need anything while you are in town.

SCENE 11

Ron is still at the church making a list for repairs. He watches Jessie walking away from the church through a patch woods and disappearing in the dense foliage. Ron is very troubled for this boy and the things he said. He remembered seeing him earlier that day going into the back of the church while he was talking to the sheriff. Ron goes in the church for the first time. Surprisingly, the old church is still standing pretty strong. There are busted windows and debris scattered about. The pews and altar seem to be sturdy and there is a beautiful painting of an angel hanging on the wall behind the minister's podium. He then goes through a door to the rooms in the back which were probably used for Sunday school classes. He looks in the first one and sees a small table with chairs and some old books and crayons laying around the floor and the table. He pushes open the next door and it is full of all kinds of different things. There are old toys and some rope. He can see an old guitar with no strings, different kinds of hats, bottles, and odd things sitting around. It looks a little like a yard sale. Somehow in all this mess it was pretty organized. He realizes this is where the little boy has been spending time and playing. Ron notices and old bible laying open on some old milk crates that the boy is using for a table. When Ron looks at the pages, he can see the picture of an angel and children all around on one page and an image of Heaven on the other. Ron leaves the room and goes outside. This boy now has his full attention.

SCENE 12

Ron and Sarah are having dinner at a restaurant in town talking and eating.

Sarah: How'd it go today? Is it going to take much for repairs and clean up?

Ron: Actually, not too bad. I am going to hire a couple of local boys to help. I have a list of things: weeds and brush need to be cut down, remove old debris from around the church, but nothing major. With help I should have it ready in a week or so.

Sarah: Well, that sounds good. Did you run into any one while you were out there?

Ron: Actually, I did. The Sheriff. Sheriff Tanner. Do you remember him? H.R. Tanner. I think that is what he said his name was.

Sarah: No I don't think so.

Ron: He said his wife used to make quilts for your mom.

Sarah: Seems like I do but it's been so long. I remember going with Mom to some lady's house and picking up quilts. I can't remember her name. Did he talk about anything else?

Ron: *(He can tell Sarah is getting a little uneasy with this conversation.)* Just typical small-town stuff and gave me the names of a couple boys that might be willing to help. Nothing much other than that. I think he was surprised to see someone on the property.

Sarah: Why is that?

Ron: He said it had been a long time since he had seen anyone around there. Then he got a call on his radio and had to leave in a hurry. There was wreck a somewhere and it sounded pretty bad.

Sarah: Oh gosh, I hope no one was hurt too bad! *(She quickly changes the subject.)* I went to the courthouse today and there are no issues. No liens or property taxes that need to be paid so we are good to go with the sale.

Ron: That's great. *(He could tell she diverted the conversation.)* Well, did you run into anyone?

Sarah: Yes, the county clerk. He was friends with my mom and dad. He came out and spoke with me a bit. Of course, he knew why we were here after seeing the deed. He said he would like to meet you before we left town.

Ron: Okay, we will for sure stop by before we leave. Hey…something interesting happened while I was visiting with the Sheriff. I kept seeing a young boy playing in the field behind the church. He was working pretty hard trying to build something right out in the middle of the field. When he was finished he attempted to climb it, but it fell apart and he fell with it!

Sarah: Oh my goodness!

Ron: I ran out there to see if he was okay and he seemed scared of me. I told him my name and he finally told me his name was Jessie.

I asked him what he was doing, and he told me he was building a ladder to try and climb to Heaven.

Sarah: That's odd.

Ron: I know.

Sarah: Of course, kids have crazy imaginations.

Ron: He looked like something was wrong with him.

Sarah: How so?

Ron: Well, he was really skinny and there were dark circles under his eyes. He looked very weak and frail.

Sarah: So, what did you do?

Ron: I helped him up and talked to him for a few minutes. I never met a kid like him before. He thought the church was an old house. The whole conversation was a little odd. Then he left. After I saw he was gone I went into the church and to the back rooms. I found a room full of all kinds of things. It looked like a yard sale but organized. On a table made from milk crates there was an old bible laying open with a picture of an angel on one page and an image of Heaven on the other. When I was talking to the boy, he said he found an old book in the church and read about Jesus and Heaven and that is why he wanted to go there. The bible I saw must be the book he is referring too.

Sarah: You think it is the boy's stuff?

Ron: Absolutely! I saw him going into the church from the back earlier while the Sheriff was there.

Sarah: Since there has been no one around he probably just made a secret hideaway for him and his buddies to hang out in.

Ron: Maybe so. Just something strange about the whole thing. Anyway, I plan to be back out there early in the morning. You want to come out awhile and see what we are getting accomplished?

Sarah: I might. I am going to be pretty busy.

Ron: With what?

Sarah: I have to find a lawyer to take care of the deed work. It needs to be transferred to you and I and then we will have to transfer to our buyers. If I get done in time I will call you. Okay?

Ron: *(Ron knows it needs to be taken care of, but he also knows she is using it to keep from going out there.)* Yeah you should probably get that started. I am sure that is not something that can be finished in a day or two.

SCENE 13

The next day Ron is at the old church waiting on two local boys he has hired to show up for work. A Blue 70's Chevy pulls up. Two boys get out of the truck and walk over to Ron.

Ron: Good morning, gentlemen! I am Ron Boggs.

Andrew: I am Andrew, and this is my brother Cole. He ain't much on talking.

Cole: Well, he ain't much on workin. *(Laughs with a shy grin.)*

Ron: *(Laughs.)* It's good to meet you boys. I appreciate you coming out on such short notice. Let me show you what I need to get done.

Andrew: What are you gonna do with this old place? I have heard stories about this old church.

Ron: We plan to sell it as soon as we can. What do you know about it?

Cole: He don't know nothin he just likes to talk. *(Laughs and knocks Andrew's ball cap off his head.)*

Andrew: Shut up, Cole!

Ron: You boys gonna be okay?

Andrew: Yeah, we just like giving each other a hard time. Sorry, Mr. Boggs.

Cole: Me too. Sorry, Mr. Boggs. Show us what you need done.

Ron shows the boys what to do and they begin working. Ron can see Jessie out behind the church.

Ron: Hey, Andrew? You know anything about that boy walking through the field behind the church?

Andrew: Not much. We see him around here a lot but that's about it. His mom and dad are kinda messed up. They don't pay any attention to him. Actually, nobody does. I think he may have something wrong with him. He looks sick. You never see him playing with any other kids. It is really kind of sad.

Ron: Cole, do you know anything about him?

Cole: Nope. Me and my dad saw him out by the road one time, and he was kicking a can. Dad stopped and gave him an old guitar he bought for ten dollars at a yard sale. It didn't have any strings, but he went down the road playing it like it did. My dad kinda felt sorry for him.

Ron: I am starting to feel the same way.

SCENE 14

Ron is watching Jessie as he makes his way to the church. He hears Jessie coughing and continues to watch him. It is a very deep, rough cough. Finally, Jessie is on his hands and knees coughing really bad. Ron starts to the field to help him. When Jessie sees him coming he gets up and starts running to the woods. Ron gets to the place where he was on his hands and knees and notices blood on the ground. Now he is convinced something is wrong with this boy. He runs to his truck and he can see glimpses of Jessie going through the woods, so Ron starts driving down the road in the direction he thinks Jessie is going. It doesn't take long before he comes up on a house and sees the boy going in the back door. Ron sits there looking around for a moment. It is a rough scene. Trash and old junk is laying around the yard. You could tell the yard was never tended too. The house is old and falling down. It is a terrible place to live. His concern for the boy causes him to get out of the truck and go to the front door. Ron knocks on the door. A woman opens the door.

Jessie's Mom: What do you want?

Ron: Mam, my name is Ron Boggs. My wife and I own the old church down the road. Your boy, Jessie, has been playing there and today—*(She cuts him off.)*

Jessie's Mom: I don't care what he has done or broke or stole or tore up! I ain't got no money so get off my porch before I call the sheriff!

Ron: No, mam, you don't understand. He hasn't done anything wrong. I saw him on his hands and knees coughing really bad earlier. When I ran out to help him he took off. I saw blood on the ground where he was coughing. So, I thought I would come and let you know so someone could take him to a doctor. He seems really sick.

Jessie's Mom: My boy ain't your business. So, you'd better be mindin' your own! Get off my porch like I said the first time.

SCENE 15

Ron realizes he is not going to get anywhere with the boy's mother. He leaves, however, he is still determined to find help for Jessie. He goes back to the church and asks Andrew about a local doctor.

Ron: Hey, Andrew, where could I find a local doctor's office? I am going to try and get help for that boy.

Andrew: There is one in town. Straight across from the library. You can't miss it.

Ron: Thanks! If I am not back before you guys quit keep up with your time and come back tomorrow at 8am.

SCENE 16

Ron is very concerned for Jessie. He arrives at the Doctors office Andrew told him about.

Ron: Excuse me, I need to see the doctor please.

Receptionist: Just fill out this form and take a seat. We will get you in as soon as we can.

Ron: Well... I am not here for me. I am here for someone else. I met this young boy recently and he seems really sick. I spoke with his mother and she does not seem too interested in bringing him to a doctor. He seems very weak and frail. Today I saw him on his hands and knees coughing. It sounded really bad and when I went to check on him, he ran away. I saw blood on the ground. Something is wrong with this kid and no one seems to care. I just want to find some help for this boy.

Receptionist: That sure don't sound good. What did you say your name was?

Ron: Ron Boggs.

Receptionist: Okay, Mr. Boggs, give me just a minute and I will see if Dr. Adler can speak with you.

Ron: Thank you!

A few moments pass and the receptionist returns.

Receptionist: Mr. Boggs. Dr. Adler will see you now.

Ron: Thank you so much! I really do appreciate it.

Receptionist: No problem. I hope the little guy gets to feeling better.

Ron steps into an office and is waiting Dr. Adler steps in the room.

Ron: Are you Dr. Adler?

Dr. Adler: Yes, sir.

Ron: Hi. My name is Ron Boggs.

Dr. Adler: Hello, Mr. Boggs, how can I help you? My receptionist mentioned something about a boy who is sick? Is it your son or grandson?

Ron: No. He is a kid who has been hanging out around an old church my wife and I just inherited. It is obvious something is wrong with him. He looks weak and pale all the time.

Dr. Adler: Are there any other symptoms that are noticeable?

Ron: Today I saw him on his knees coughing. It sounded really deep and rough. When I went to check on him, he got up and ran a way. I looked down and saw blood on the ground.

Dr. Adler: Oh Goodness! He does sound sick. If you can get someone to bring him to the clinic, I can check him out and try to help.

Ron: That will probably be an issue. His mother all but threw me off their porch and said it was none of my business. I can't understand why she would not want to help her own child.

Dr. Adler: Unfortunately, there are a lot of parents in this world who react too slow to child illness and it is the kids that pay the price. Do you know the mother's name?

Ron: No she didn't say.

Dr. Adler: Where exactly is their house?

Ron: If you go past the old church it's the second house on the right about a quarter of a mile down the road. It's a pretty rough scene to look at.

Dr. Adler: I know who you are talking about. The boy's mother's name is Lyla. When she was pregnant with him, I was treating her for an illness. After he was born, I never saw her again. She just quit coming for her treatments.

Ron: What type of illness did she have?

Dr. Adler: I'm sorry, Mr. Boggs, but I can't disclose patient information. I really have said too much already. I truly wish there was something I could do to help. Like I said if you can get his mother to agree for you or someone to bring him in, I can get him some help.

Ron: I understand. It is just so hard to see a kid suffer like that and not be able to do anything about it.

Dr. Adler: I know it is a tragedy what some kids have to go through because of parents who simply don't care. Have you been to child services? They may be able to help.

Ron: Thank you for your time, Dr. Adler. I will check with child services first. I don't think I will make much progress with the mother.

Dr. Adler: Good Luck, Mr. Boggs

Ron: Thanks again for your time.

SCENE 17

Four teenage girls are walking down the street passing out flyers.

Bri: This is crap! It's twenty degrees outside, we are on Christmas vacation, and we are wasting our time passing out stupid flyers! What are these anyway? A bake sale or something?

Sarah Beth: Oh, come on, Bri! This is fun! We are letting everyone know about the lighting of the Hopetown Christmas tree. Besides there are lots of cute boys out shoveling snow today. Like that one right there! *(Sarah noticing a young man shoveling off the side walk.)*

Chelsea: Listen! We all agreed to do this. It may not mean much to us but it's a big deal for a lot people. Not to mention we are all getting paid. I don't know about you guys, but I could use the extra money!

Jannah: Hey, if you guys can score some *really* good eggnog…*(Jannah has mischievous look on her face.)* I will stay out here all day! *(Laughing.)*

An Elderly Gentlemen comes walking by.

Bri: Excuse me, sir. We would like to invite you to the lighting of the Hopetown Christmas tree. There will be carolers, elves, Santa Claus, the works. You definitely don't want to miss this. Make sure and bring this flyer with you and you will get a free hot cocoa or coffee! *(Really big smile.)*

Elderly man: Well, thank you, young lady. It's refreshing to see someone your age with such enthusiasm about her hometown events. I will do my best to make it. You girls have a nice day. *(Pauses.)* Hey…one more thing. The rest of you should let a little of her holiday cheer rub off on you. *(Smiles and waves.)* Happy Holidays!

Chelsea: Well now! Aren't you Miss Holiday Cheer Captain. *(Laughs.)*

Bri: I am not a Scrooge! I just can't stand walking around in a deep freeze! *(Sassy.)* Besides I can be charming when I want to be!

Jannah: A bit over the top but I believe he was sold on the idea. *(Grinning and laughing.)*

Sarah Beth: Way to go, Bri! See this can be fun!

Jannah: Dear lord, Sarah, you would have a good time barefoot in a blizzard! *(Laughing.)*

Sarah Beth Sticks her tongue out at Jannah.

Chelsea: Seriously! *(Laughing.)* Good job, Bri! Now let's spread the holiday cheer!! Fa la, la, la, la, la, la, la, la. *(Being silly and with joyful laughter.)*

All Four girls continue passing out the flyers and having a good time with each other.

SCENE 18

Sarah is at the bed and breakfast. She is setting up a site to post the Church property for sale. She can hear pots clanging and hear Alberta singing downstairs. She closes her eyes and reminisces of Christmases she spent helping her mama prepare dinner for their family. Deep in her own thoughts she finds herself in her mama's kitchen. Nat King Cole is singing The Christmas Song on the radio. Her dad is sitting by a blazing fire, visiting with family. The smell of vanilla, cinnamon, and hazelnut fills the house. A knock on the door interrupts her daydream.

Alberta: Sarah? Are you here, honey?

Sarah: *(Sarah opens the door. It is obvious she has been crying.)* Yes. Oh, hello, Alberta *(Smiling and wiping away her tears.)*

Alberta: *(Smiling, not letting on she notices.)* Sweetie, would you like to come downstairs and help me in the kitchen? I am fixing a big Christmas dinner for all our guests and I could sure use the company.

Sarah: That sounds nice. I will be right down.

Sarah and Alberta are in the kitchen. Alberta is rolling out dough on the counter. Preparing to fix her famous chicken and dumplings.

Alberta: Sarah, did your mama ever make chicken and dumplings?

Sarah: She did but not like this. I have never seen someone cut the dough in little squares like that before.

Alberta: It's a lot of work but that's the way Ted likes it. Not to mention all the grandkids! Lord I've never seen anything like it in my life! Those little ones will line up with bowls and a spoon like little birds waiting for a worm.

Sarah: Oh, that's so sweet! How many grandkids do you have?

Ted: Bert, have you got those dumplings ready?

Alberta: Now, Ted, I will have them done when I get them done. *(Smiles at Sarah.)*

Ted: Ok, Bert.

Sarah: Sounds like somebody is getting anxious.

Alberta: *(She winks a Sarah.)* He knows I always give him the first helping after I am finished.

Sarah: You two seem so close. How long have you and Ted been together?

Alberta: Over sixty years.

Sarah: Wow! That's amazing!

Alberta: Always remember, Sarah, a good bowl of dumplings and a whole lot a loving will keep a man happy and at home. *(Both laugh.)*

Alberta: Oh, back to your question about how many grandkids I have. I have two daughters, five grandchildren, twelve great grandchildren and five great-great-grandchildren.

Sarah: That's wonderful! Do they come here for Christmas?

Alberta: Most of them do. Sometimes jobs and other families keep them away but that's the way it goes when they grow up and get married. Do you and Ron have any children?

Sarah: *(Gets kinda of somber for a second.)* No. We never did. We thought about it but we both were pretty driven by our careers and then time kinda slipped by before we knew it. *(Awkward silence for a moment.)* So, did any of your granddaughters ever master the art of your famous dumplings?

Alberta: Well, before I respond to that I will have to say I love all of them and they are all special in their own way. But my daughter Peggy's oldest girl, Teddi Leigh, is the one. From the time she was a little girl she would stand on a bucket beside me and I would show her how to do it. I remember the first time I let her knead the dough. Her little hands could barely do it, but she was determined to be like her mamaw. She worked so hard she would break a sweat. She would say, "Mamaw, is this right? Mamaw, how long do I have to do this before its ready? Mamaw, why do they call it kneading anyway? They oughta call it squishing!" Then she would laugh like she had said the funniest thing on this earth.

Sarah: Sounds like she is her mamaw's little clone. Where is she now?

Alberta: She is in Kentucky and spends a lot of time in Nashville, Tennessee. She married a Cyrus boy from up there and he writes songs and she sings 'em. They seem to do alright. I believe she hooked him with these dumplings.

Both laugh.

Sarah: *(Somber.)* Alberta, I want to thank you for this. When you came to my door earlier, I was having a moment. This has really helped. Losing Mom has been really hard.

Alberta: It's hard to lose your mama, child. I remember when my mother passed away. I thought I would never be able to get over it. You know what... I never did! But I learned how to live with it. I quickly found out she is still here with me. Every time I start rolling out the dough for these dumplings, I can feel her hands guiding mine just like she did when I was a little girl. *(She puts her hand on Sara's face affectionately)* Sweetie, she will always be a part of you because you are a part of her.

Sarah hugs Alberta.

Sarah: You are just what I needed, Alberta!

Alberta: There has been a lot of tears dried and broken hearts mended in this old kitchen. God always knows what we need and when we need it. He is always right on time.

SCENE 19

Ron went to the child welfare department after visiting the doctor to no avail. Sarah calls Ron.

Ron: Hey, honey.

Sarah: Hey, Alberta is fixing a Christmas dinner for the guests at the bed and breakfast. It looks amazing!

Ron: Sounds good. Sarah…*(Sarah is waiting on what he is going to say for a moment.)*

Sarah: Are you still there?

Ron: I'm here…

Sarah: What's wrong, Ron?

Ron: Do you remember the boy I told you about?

Sarah: You mean the boy that has been playing in the church?

Ron: Yes. Sarah, there is something wrong with him. He is really sick.

Sarah: That's terrible. Well, I hope he is okay. Sounds like you are really bothered about this.

Ron: I just wish I could help him.

Sarah: I am sure if he is that sick him parents will take him to the doctor. Are you on your way?

Ron knows Sarah truly does not realize the situation with Jessie.

Ron: I should be there is a few minutes.

Sarah: Okay great! I think dinner is about ready! See ya soon.

Ron: Sarah...

Sarah already disconnected.

SCENE 20

The next morning Ron is at the church. Andrew and Cole are working. As the day passes Ron watches for Jessie. In the afternoon he can see him coming through the field and disappears in the back of the church. Ron continues to work but always watching. Jessie stays out of sight for a long time. He is getting a little concerned. Then he sees him running and laughing flapping his arms like a bird. Andrew and Cole notice Jessie as well. All three stop what they are doing. Jessie is running all over the field and flapping his arms.

Cole: He has lost his mind!

Andrew: There is definitely something wrong with that boy. Ron, you should have went to see another kind of doctor.

Ron: *(Watching very intently.)* No… He has been reading a book he found in the church. He doesn't know it's a bible.

Cole: Are you serious? Who doesn't know what a bible is?

Andrew: Well, I am surprised you do, Cole. You don't ever open yours.

Cole: Well, at least if I did, I could actually read.

Ron: You two are like a comedy show. *(Laughs. Ron is very focused on Jessie and what he is doing)* He has figured out how to get there...

Ron continues to watch Jessie in a bit of wonderment. Andrew and Cole go back to their work.

Scene 21

That evening Hopetown was having their annual lighting of the town Christmas tree. Christmas was only a few days away. This is the big event in Hopetown. Everybody shows up! Ron and Sarah walk down town to check out the festivities.

Sarah: This is amazing! Look at all the lights.

Ron: I know. You never think that all these people actually live here.

Sarah: Look, Ron! They have a real sleigh for Santa! Is that horse tied to it?

Ron: Maybe ol' Donner and Blitzen retired. *(Laughs.)*

Sarah: *(Punching Ron playfully and laughing.)* Real funny. I think it's cute.

Ron: Hopetown really takes their decorating seriously!

Sarah: You remember the first night we were here?

Ron: Yeah and we both noticed there wasn't a nativity scene or any kind of religious reference to the holiday.

Sarah: I was really young, but Hopetown was always a bible-belt town.

Sheriff Tanner: Hey Ron good to see you again.

They shake hands.

Ron: Sarah, this is Sheriff Tanner.

Sarah: Really good to meet you.

Sheriff Tanner: Ron tells me your mama passed away.

Sarah: Yeah she was sick for a long time.

Sherriff Tanner: I sure hate to hear that. You know I remember you like it was yesterday. Your mama would come by our house to get quilts my wife would sew for her. You would head straight out to my barn wanting to see the horses.

Sarah: I remember. One of those horses was named Sam.

Sherriff Tanner: That's right. Boy what a character he was. Ron, that horse was like a human. He would take his mouth and unlock his stall door. Then he would let the rest of them out. I never could get mad at him though. He was just being mischievous like a young boy.

Ron: Sounds like he was a handful.

Sheriff Tanner: Well, he was at times, but he was a big part of the family. I guess I had better let you two enjoy your evening. Good to see you again, Sarah, and nice to have you back. Ron, I will catch up with you and finish that story I started the other day. *(Sheriff winks and smiles at Ron.)*

Ron: Sounds good. You know where to find me. *(Ron is looking to see Sarah's reaction.)*

Sarah: What story is he talking about?

Ron: Oh he was going on about some tale about some boys who used to stir up trouble around here. Then he got a call on his radio and had to leave before he could finish. You know how old men love to tell stories. You get about ten percent of what really happened. *(Laughing.)*

She just smiles. Ron can tell she is bothered a little. Whatever happened in that old church must have been pretty bad because she keeps it locked deep inside.

Sarah: Hey, I am a little tired and cold. You seen enough?

Ron: Yeah me too. Besides I wanna get out there early tomorrow and finish up.

Ron puts his arm around Sarah as they walk back to the Bed and Breakfast.

Sarah: You want me to go ahead and post it? I have all the information loaded.

Ron: I don't see why not. I will send you a few pics when I get out there. It looks a whole lot better than the ones I sent when I first started.

Sarah: I am glad we did this tonight. It was fun.

Ron pulls her close and kisses her forehead.

Ron: Me too.

SCENE 22

The next day Ron is at the church early putting the finishing touches on the property. Later in the afternoon he is finished and is getting a "for sale" sign out of the back of his truck. He gets his hammer and starts pounding the sign in the ground. He looks up and is startled by Jessie standing there watching him.

Ron: Jessie, you scared me to death. *(Laughs.)*

Jessie: *(Jessie has a serious look on his face)* Mr. Boggs, are you going to sell this place?

Ron: Yes, Jessie. That's why my wife and I came here.

Tears begin to fill up Jessie's eyes. He is getting very emotional and lashes out at Ron.

Jessie: What will I do? That "church," as you call it, is the only place I have to go. My daddy stays drunk and is always gone. My mama acts like she hates me all the time. Everything that happens is my fault. When they start fighting this is the only place I have to hide to get away from them. Besides all my things I have collected are in there. What will I do with them? It's all I have! You can't sell it, Mr. Boggs!

Ron: Jessie, I am sorry but—

Jessie: *(Jessie is very upset and crying and mad)* You're not sorry! You're just like all grownups. "Get out of my way, little kid. I don't have time for you. I wish you were never born." I thought you were my friend. You were the only person that ever wanted to talk to me and ask me anything. Other kids won't even play with me because I am poor, and they think I have something wrong me.

Ron tries to hold Jessie.

Jessie: Get away from me! I hate you! It don't matter anyway! When Jesus sends me my wings, I am going to fly to Heaven and nobody will ever have to be bothered with me again!

Jessie takes off running. He falls several times because he is so weak. Ron walks towards him but Jessie won't let him help. Ron sits down on the ground and becomes emotional. He feels helpless and defeated. After a few minutes he gathers himself and gets in his truck. As he drives, he hears every word Jessie said to him over and over. He is completely devastated.

SCENE 23

Sarah is back at the bed and breakfast. She just posted the property online and already has a response. Her cell phone rings.

Sarah: Hello?

Caller: Hi my name is Bud Shirkey. I am the Vice President of Flatwoods Oil Company. I saw your posting online for the property in Hopetown, Virginia. We are very interested. Who may I ask am I speaking with?

Sarah: My name is Sarah Boggs. I am little surprised to get a call this quick.

Caller: Well, Mrs. Boggs, we have been watching that area for a long time. We have gas and food marts all over Virginia and Kentucky. Hopetown is predicted to boom since they built the new four-lane. According to the Virginia Highway Department your property is right beside the new exit into Hopetown.

Sarah: I had no idea! *(Laughing.)* Had I known I would have increased the asking price.

Caller: *(Laughs.)* That won't be necessary, Mrs. Boggs. I think you will find our offer satisfactory.

Sarah: Okay you have my attention, Mr. Shirkey.

Caller: My company will pay you twice the amount for your property if you immediately take it off the Internet sites. Furthermore, we asked that you dispose of any advertisement that you have generated. I am prepared to wire you half of the offer today if you will accept.

Sarah: Mr. Shirkey, I am speechless. I am sure we will accept your offer. However, I need to speak with my husband about this before I commit. He is actually at the property as we speak. Let me try to reach him and I will call you right back.

Caller: Okay, Mrs. Boggs, I will be waiting for your call.

Sarah: It shouldn't take very long. I know my husband is going to be very excited about this! I will call soon! Thanks so much!

Caller: We thank you, mam. Talk soon.

Sarah tries to call Ron. She hears a phone ringing. She then realizes he left his phone on the dresser when he left this morning. She calls Mr. Shirkey back

Caller: This is Bud Shirkey. How can I help you?

Sarah: Mr. Shirkey, it's Sarah Boggs.

Caller: Well, hello, Mrs. Boggs, that was quick. Was your husband pleased with my offer?

Sarah: I tried calling him and heard his phone ringing. He left it on the dresser so I am going to have to wait till he comes back before I can speak with him. I am so sorry!

Caller: I totally understand. Just call me as soon as you have a chance to speak with him. It is getting late in the day so I may not be able to wire the earnest money today and tomorrow, of course, is Christmas Eve. So, if you both decide to accept then it would be after Christmas before I could transfer any funds.

Sarah: Mr. Shirkey, that is not a problem. I am sure Ron will want to do this and we will not need the earnest money to stop the advertising. We will deal with that after Christmas.

Caller: I look forward to your call.

Sarah: Thanks again, Mr. Shirkey!

SCENE 24

Ron is at Jessie's house but does not get out of his truck. He just sits there for a few moments. He feels so helpless. He knows Jessie is very sick and there is nothing he can do for him. Now he has broken his heart and is taking away the only refuge he has on this earth. Ron is totally distraught. He begins to drive to the bed and breakfast. As he is driving, he looks for his phone to call Sarah and tell her about what happened with Jessie. He can't find it. He pulls over thinking it may have fell in the floorboard. He becomes frustrated looking for the phone. He slips on some loose gravel on the shoulder of the road and falls down an embankment. He stands up and dusts himself off. The fall interrupted his frustration trying to find his phone. He looks up.

Ron: All my Life I have been able to handle anything you have thrown at me! But—*(Ron begins to cry, continuing to look up)* But I am lost on this one. I truly thought you set this up so we could have the extra money to invest in our business and not have to take it from our retirement. When we found out Judy left this church to us it just made sense at the time. So much that I didn't even question Sarah about not ever telling me she was from Hopetown. Am I wrong? Is there something I am not seeing here? For the first time in my life I really don't know what to do or how to fix this. Why am I here? For Jessie, the church, Sarah, What? Whatever it is please show me. Please! I know there has to be a reason for all this but right now I feel completely defeated and confused.

Ron gets back in his truck and heads to the bed and breakfast. He has no idea what Sarah is about to tell him, and she has no idea what Ron is dealing with. She is on a cloud with her excitement about the phone call and he is in a deep valley and very torn about selling the church property.

SCENE 25

Ron arrives and comes through the front door of the bed and breakfast. Sarah comes bouncing down the stairs.

Sarah: Hey, I have been trying to call you, but you left your phone on the dresser.

Ron: I was wondering what I did with it. I was looking for it earlier to call you.

Sarah: Anyway, you are never going to believe what happened. I went ahead and posted pics of the property you took the other day with the details about the place and our asking price. Less than hour ago I got a call from a Mr. Shirkey. He is a VP for Flatwood Oil Company. Long story short he has offered us twice our asking price! I was speechless.

Ron: Why would he do that?

Sarah: He said they wanted it before anyone could get their hands on it and requested we take down all advertising as soon as we agree to the deal. He also said he would wire us half of his offer today. But, of course, the banks are closed already so he would have to send it after Christmas. I was blown away. I told him I am sure you would absolutely be great with the offer, but I wanted to discuss it with you first. You are okay with this aren't you?

Ron: Yeah that sounds great. We will uh…just…get our attorney to start the paperwork after Christmas. *(Sarah's excitement is deflated by Ron's reaction.)*

Sarah: Ron, I figured you would be bouncing off the walls with this news? What's wrong?

Ron: Nothing. I think it's great news. That's awesome, Sarah.

(Ron is trying to rally for Sarah but she doesn't buy it. He turns and walks out on the front porch and sits down in a rocking chair. He leans over with his face in his hands when Sarah comes out strong and the screen door slams behind her. Ron stays motionless.)

Sarah: This is twice in one day that I am blown away. I can't believe this! You were the one who wanted to come here in the first place! You said, "Sarah, this will be great for us! This could be a God send! We can sell this property and start our business with the money, and we won't have to touch our retirement or savings!" Now I tell you we have an offer for twice the amount and you say, "That's great, Sarah. That's awesome, Sarah," and then turn around and walk out! What's wrong, Ron? Why have you changed?

Ron: *(Ron looks up at Sarah in anguish.)* Sarah, it's the boy.

Sarah: What boy?

Ron: Jessie, the kid I told you about that has been playing in the church. He is real sick, Sarah, and no one seems to care. The church is the only refuge he has to escape the hell he lives in.

Sarah: What are you saying? Have you changed your mind about selling?

Ron: Sarah, I don't know what to do!

Sarah: Ron, I can't believe this! I don't know you right now!

Sarah is upset and takes off down the porch and goes around behind the bed and breakfast and into the back yard. Ron gets up and follows her onto the back yard.

Ron: Sarah, wait a minute! You say you don't know me? For the last twenty-six years I have been married to a wife I thought I knew everything about until the other day when the attorney handed you the deed. You were so disturbed by it that you couldn't get out of his office quick enough. Every time we mention that old church people seem very awkward and uncomfortable. You have dodged every time I have asked you to go out there. You change the subject every time it's brought up! Sarah, please tell me!

Sarah: Ron, I don't want to talk about this right now!

Ron: Do I have to wait another twenty-six years to find out about this? You know I came here with one goal. To sell this property and go home, buy a charter boat, and spend more time with you and supplement our retirement. Since I came here all that has changed. I don't think we are here by accident. I don't think we are here for the reasons we came. I think there is something much bigger going on! *(Sarah is starting to cry and looking down. Ron puts his hands gently on her face.)* Sarah, look at me. Please... *(Sarah looks at Ron.)* Talk to me. Get rid of this! You can't continue to harbor this burden any longer. It is going to destroy you inside. Sarah, I believe that your mother left this church to you for a reason. I know what I said before but things have changed! I have changed. Talk to me.

Sarah: *(Emotional and crying.)* Ron... It's so hard to talk about... (Ron still has his hands on her face trying to tenderly keep her attention.)

Ron: I got you. *(Wiping tears as they fall and looking deep in her eyes)* I love you so much, Sarah. Open up to me. Please!

Sarah: My Grandfather was...

Ron: Come on. It's okay.

Sarah becoming more emotional and crying harder. Ron is patient.

Sarah: He was... Ron...

Sarah: (Sarah pulls away.) I can't do this!

Ron: Yes, you can! *(Touching her face again. He knows she has to let this out. Ron is beginning to understand why God brought them here.)* Sarah, look at me. This is why we are here.

Sarah: Why?

Ron: Change and Healing. It is so clear to me now. You and me, this town, Jessie, the church...it's all a part of why we are here. Sarah. Sarah, talk to me. What happened to your grandfather?

Sarah: My grandfather was...he died in the church!

Sarah completely breaks down crying. Years of hurt bottled up comes out in a river of tears. Ron holds her. Sarah is calming down and starts to tell Ron what happened.

Sarah: My grandfather built the church before I was born. He was a pillar in this community. He always said that Hopetown was a place of Hope and healing. That when people came here, they were never the same after they left.

Ron: I agree with your grandfather.

Sarah: The church was always full. He was very protective of the members of the church. If anyone was in need or sick, he would always be there to help. Mrs. Thompson was a widow who had been a member of the church since it was built. There was a family that lived down the road from her. There were six boys and their father. Their mother had died giving birth to the youngest one. They were all trouble. They would steal from Mrs. Thompson and drive their trucks through her garden and kept her in fear. She would call the sheriff, but mom said the sheriff was a cousin and would not do anything to stop them. He would just act like they were harmless. My grandfather decided to go to their house and talk to them and ask them to leave her alone. He was standing on the porch talking to two of the brothers and things got heated. Mom always said that, although he was a preacher, he would stand his ground for the right cause. Well, they were arguing and a third brother came through the house and tried to shoot my grandfather through the screen door.

He hit his brother instead and killed him. My grandfather ran to his truck and got away from their house. He called the sheriff and told him what happened. The sheriff told him he would handle it and would be in touch to fill out a report. Two days later Sunday service had just started, and the doors flung open to the church. It sounded like thunder! I was so scared! I was sitting on the front pew beside my mother. It was the boy's father Mr. Johnson. As he walked towards the pulpit my grandfather said, "Mr. Johnson, I know why you are here. I am sorry for the loss of your son. I only went out there to ask them to leave Mrs. Thompson alone and your boys became violent." Mr. Johnson raised the gun and shot my grandfather. *(Sarah is emotional and starting to cry.)*

Ron: *(Holds her.)* Sarah, I am so sorry! Oh my gosh!

Sarah: The next week we moved to Charleston.

Sarah is still emotional and crying. Ron is still holding her.

Ron: Sarah. we can't sell the church.

Sarah: *(Starts to smile with tears.)* I know… I know…

SCENE 26

The next day is Christmas Eve. Ron is rushing to get out to the church and take down the sign and tell Jessie. Sarah is going to let Mr. Shirkey know they are not selling. When Ron arrives at the church, he doesn't see Jessie anywhere. He gets out of his truck and yells for him. He opens the door of the church and calls for him but no response. He is now getting concerned. The moment he had with Jessie yesterday is ringing in his head. Ron decides to go to the boy's house. He knows it will be a confrontation, but he needs to know Jessie is okay and wants to tell him the good news.

Jessie's Mother: I thought I told you to stay away from here?

Ron: I just want to know if Jessie is home.

Jessie's Mother: I don't care what you want. Get out of here, Mr. Church Man

Ron: Can you just for one second act like you have a child that you care about and tell me if he is home or not.

Jessie's Mother: He ain't been here all day. He is probably down there at your old church house. He was talking some crazy talk about Jesus going send him wings for Christmas so he could fly to Heaven. *(Ron starts quickly to his truck and the mother is yelling at Ron as he leaves.)* I don't know what kind of crazy things you put in his head, Church Man, but you better leave him alone. He ain't none of your concern.

Ron calls Sarah.

Ron: Sarah, I can't find Jessie.

Sarah: Come and get me. I will help you look.

SCENE 27

(Ron picks Sarah up at the bed and breakfast.)

Sarah: Did you check his house?

Ron: Yeah, I did and he wasn't there.

Sarah: Did you talk to his mother?

Ron: You could call it that. *They drive around looking in the community and no sign of Jessie.* He has to be at the church. Sarah, he was really upset when he found out we were selling and I noticed the last few days that he looks much worse.

Sarah: I hope he is okay.

Ron: Me too…

They arrive at the church.

Ron: *(Jumps out.)* I am going to check the woods that go from here to his house. Go in the church and see if he is hiding somewhere. *(Ron is running towards the woods.)*

Sarah is in a trance staring at the front doors of the church. You can see the terror on her face. She walks slowly to the front door. You can hear faint sounds of Ron calling for Jessie. Everything is focused on Sarah. As she pushes the doors open, she begins to recall the day her grandfather was shot. She can see Mr. Johnson and hear the doors fling open. As she begins to walk up the aisle, she can see him walking up the aisle. Back and forth from recollection to now. She is taking each step as he did. That slow determined walk he took to commit his crime.

As she gets closer to the pulpit where her grandfather fell to the floor, she can see still see the blood stain where he was laying after he was shot. Back and forth in her mind, her visions are so dramatic and real. She moves behind the pulpit and hears the gun shot that killed her grandfather. Then, like instant silence and peace, she looks down to see Jessie, folded up and lifeless, under the pulpit, holding that old bible he has been reading. She begins to yell for Ron. She is crying.

Sarah: Ron, Ron, Ron. I found him! *(Sarah crouches down and speaks to Jessie.)* Jessie, I am Sarah, Ron's wife.

Jessie: *(He is so weak but smiles.)* Where's Ron?

Sarah: He will be here in just a minute.

Jessie: I get my wings today.

Sarah: What did you say, Jessie?

Jessie: Jesus said I would get my wings today. *(Jessie has a weak smile on his face.)*

Sarah: *(Sarah hears Ron coming in.)* Ron, hurry he is right here.

Ron moves behind the pulpit and can see Jessie. He carefully unfolds him one arm at a time and cradles him in his arms. The whole time Jessie keeps holding his bible. Ron sits down with him on the front pew and Sarah is standing with her hands on her face crying.

Jessie: Merry Christmas, Ron. *(With a sweet smile Jessie takes his last breath in peace.)*

Ron: *(He begins to cry.)* Merry Christmas to you too, buddy.

The song Send Me Wings written and performed by Bobby Cyrus will begin.

During this you will see scenes of people gathering outside the church. You will see shots of Jessie running through the field, pretending to fly. You will see characters you saw throughout the story. Also, an ambulance, coroner, and sheriff vehicles in front of the church. As the song comes to a close the screen should go black for a moment, giving the viewer the sense that the movie is over. Then across the screen reads "One year later." You begin to hear a church choir singing the old gospel song, "I'll Fly Away." Then you will see a blue sky with beautiful puffy white clouds. A breeze will gently rustle leaves on the trees as the singing becomes louder and louder until, in an instant, you are in the church. Ron and Sarah have completely brought the church back to its original state when it was built by her grandfather years ago.

You will see all kinds of familiar faces in the congregation. Jessie's mother is sitting on the back per, holding the old. Ragged bible in her lap. She has his name and wings wrapped around it tattooed on her arm. The visual goes outside to the front doors of the church and slowly rises to reveal the name on the Church.

Jessie's Hopetown Chapel

God's House of Hope and Healing

The End

About the Author

Bobby Cyrus is from Louisa, a small town in east Kentucky. He has spent over thirty years as a writer, musician, singer, and producer with songs recorded by Gospel, Bluegrass, and Country artists. He is very humbled by these gifts and gives all the credit for anything he accomplishes to God.